Shapes Everywhere

Shapes at School

Oona Gaarder-Juntti
Consulting Editor, Diane Craig, M.A./Reading Specialist

A Division of ABDO

ABDO
Publishing Company

visit us at www.abdopublishing.com

Published by ABDO Publishing Company, a division of ABDO, P.O. Box 398166, Minneapolis, Minnesota 55439.

Printed in the United States of America, North Mankato, Minnesota
062013
092013

 PRINTED ON RECYCLED PAPER

Editor: Liz Salzmann
Content Developer: Nancy Tuminelly
Cover and Interior Design and Production: Oona Gaarder-Juntti, Mighty Media, Inc.
Photo Credits: Ablestock.com, Brand X Pictures, Comstock, Creatas Images, Hemera Technologies, Jupiterimages, PhotoObjects.net, Shutterstock, Stockbyte, Thinkstock

Library of Congress Cataloging-in-Publication Data
Gaarder-Juntti, Oona, 1979-
  Shapes at school / Oona Gaarder-Juntti.
      p. cm. -- (Shapes everywhere)
  ISBN 978-1-61783-412-7
  1. Shapes--Juvenile literature. 2. Schools--Juvenile literature. I. Title.
  QA445.5.G338 2013
  516'.15--dc23
                          2011051110

Super SandCastle™ books are created by a team of professional educators, reading specialists, and content developers around five essential components—phonemic awareness, phonics, vocabulary, text comprehension, and fluency—to assist young readers as they develop reading skills and strategies and increase their general knowledge. All books are written, reviewed, and leveled for guided reading, early reading intervention, and Accelerated Reader® programs for use in shared, guided, and independent reading and writing activities to support a balanced approach to literacy instruction.

Table of Contents

Shapes Are Everywhere

Shapes are everywhere at school! Here are some shapes you might see. Let's learn more about shapes.

2-D or 3-D?

2-Dimensional Shapes

Some shapes are two-dimensional,
or 2-D. A 2-D shape is flat.
You can draw it on a piece of paper.

circle
2-D shape

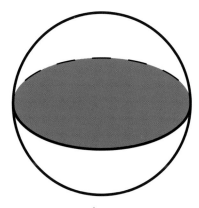

sphere
3-D shape

3-Dimensional Shapes

Some shapes are three-dimensional,
or 3-D. A 3-D shape takes up space.
You can hold a 3-D shape in your hands.

RECTANGLE

A book is a rectangle. Michael likes to go to the school **library**. He checks out new books every Friday. He loves to read books about **cowboys**.

SQUARE

The computer keys are square. Emily does her homework on a computer. She is writing a report. It is about her summer vacation.

The United States flag has 50 stars. There is a star for each state. Olivia's class says the **Pledge of Allegiance** every morning.

The **tuba's** bell is a circle. Madison watches her brother play in the marching band. The band plays during halftime.

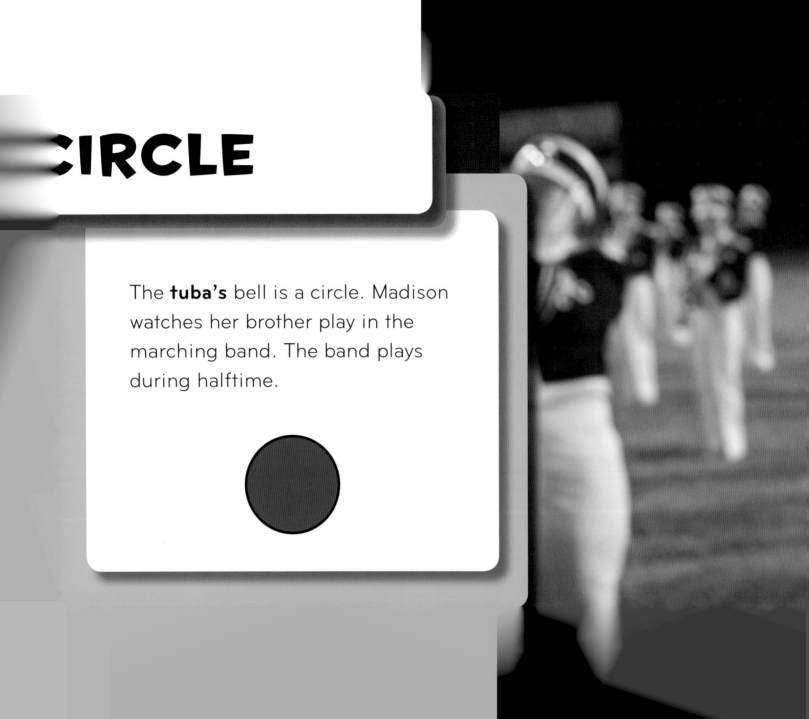

SPHERE

A basketball is a sphere. Dylan's class plays basketball in the gym. After class Dylan helps put the basketballs away.

CONE

The tip of the pencil is a cone. Jack has a math **test** today. He sharpens his pencils before the test.

TRIANGLE

The **sandwich** is cut into two triangles. Rachel brings her lunch to school. Today she has a peanut butter and jelly sandwich.

OCTAGON

The stop sign is an octagon. An octagon has eight sides. George stays after school to play soccer. He rides a school bus home after practice.

Shapes!

Here are the shapes in this book, plus a few more.
Look for them when you are at school!

diamond

rectangle

pentagon

hexagon

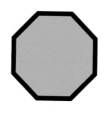

octagon

square

star

heart

oval

triangle

circle

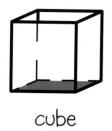

cube

sphere

cylinder

cone

pyramid

How Many?

How many shapes can you find in this picture?

Glossary

cowboy – someone who raises or takes care of horses or cattle.

library – a place that has books, CDs, magazines, newspapers, and other materials that people can use or borrow.

pledge – a promise or agreement. The Pledge of Allegiance is a statement people say that promises loyalty to the United States.

sandwich – two pieces of bread with a filling, such as meat, cheese, or peanut butter, between them.

test – an activity that shows how much someone has learned about something.

tuba – a large, brass musical instrument.